THIS PLAYBOOK BELONGS TO:

_____

MIGHTY
MINI
PRESS

"And so the adventure **begins...**"

BE **CREATIVE**

Let's warm up!

List five things that are the same color.

1. _____

2. _____

3. _____

4. _____

5. _____

List five things that start with the letter S.

1. _____

2. _____

3. _____

4. _____

5. _____

BE **CREATIVE**

List five things that are hot.

1. _____

2. _____

3. _____

4. _____

5. _____

List five things that grow.

1. _____

2. _____

3. _____

4. _____

5. _____

List five things that are free.

1. _____

2. _____

3. _____

4. _____

5. _____

BE **CREATIVE**

Write a poem that is 20 words and four lines long.

_____

_____

_____

_____

Choose a color.
Go for a stroll and notice wherever you see that color
(it might be useful to bring a pen and paper). When you
get back, write for ten minutes about the things you saw.

_____

_____

_____

_____

_____

_____

_____

_____

_____

_____

BE **CREATIVE**

Look around your room (or out the window) and write
a short description about five objects.

_____

_____

_____

_____

_____

_____

_____

_____

Go to Twitter, Facebook or Instagram and
write about the first post you see in two or three sentences.

_____

_____

_____

_____

_____

_____

BE **CREATIVE**

Write a six-word memoir. For example: Eat. Drink.
Sleep. Laugh. Cry. Die.

_____

If you were given five extra hours today and you weren't
allowed to use them for "normal things"
(e.g. eating, sleeping, etc.),what would you do with them?
Spend at least 15 minutes writing about this.

_____

_____

_____

_____

_____

_____

_____

_____

_____

_____

_____

_____

BE **CREATIVE**

You live on an abandoned island. Describe your day in
at least six sentences.

_____

_____

_____

_____

_____

_____

_____

_____

_____

_____

_____

_____

_____

_____

BE **CREATIVE**

What's the best thing that's ever happened to you?
Write as many sentences as you can in five minutes.

_____

_____

_____

_____

_____

_____

_____

_____

_____

_____

_____

_____

_____

_____

_____

BE **CREATIVE**

You have 10 days to live. In 5-10 sentences,
what would you do?

_____

_____

_____

_____

_____

_____

_____

_____

_____

_____

_____

_____

_____

_____

BE **COLORFUL**

Color these mandalas to help you relax and be more present.

BE **COLORFUL**

Color these mandalas to help you relax and be more present.

BE **COLORFUL**

Color these mandalas to help you relax and be more present.

BE **COLORFUL**

Color these mandalas to help you relax and be more present.

"**Adventure**
may hurt you
but
monotony will kill you."
– Unknown

BE **PLAYFUL**

Fill the empty squares so that each number appears
exactly once in every row, column and box.

5		2	6	7			9	
				3		4		
			4	8		7		6
	7			6				
3		1				9		4
				5			1	
1		8		9	2			
		7		4				
	9			1	6	8		2

BE **PLAYFUL**

Fill the empty squares so that each number appears
exactly once in every row, column and box.

			5	2			9	
		7				4		5
6	5						8	
					7	9	2	4
7			2		5			8
9	2	3	6					
	7						1	6
4		1				3		
	9			3	1			

BE **PLAYFUL**

Fill the empty squares so that each number appears
exactly once in every row, column and box.

				8			1	6
4		8		2				
		3	5			9		
		6	2		1	8	9	
3								2
	8	9	3		5	4		
		5			4	3		
				5		6		9
7	4			3				

BE **PLAYFUL**

Fill the empty squares so that each number appears
exactly once in every row, column and box.

	2					6		
6					7	1		3
				6	1		2	
9	7				2	4		5
			7		9			
2		5	6				7	8
	3		1	9				
5		8	2					1
		6					5	

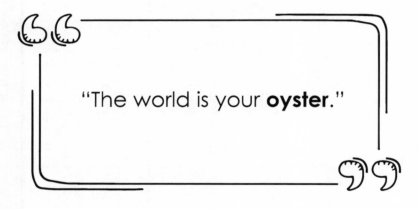

"The world is your **oyster**."

BE **PLAYFUL**

Find a path from the entrance to the exit without hitting any dead ends.

BE **PLAYFUL**

Find a path from the entrance to the exit without hitting any dead ends.

BE **PLAYFUL**

Find a path from the entrance to the exit without hitting any dead ends.

"Travel
and
change of place
impart new vigor to the mind."
- Seneca

ANAGRAMS

Simply unscramble the words.

Inspirational Phrases

JOCOSE HOY _____

AVER EBB _____

YULE OVAL YORE _____

GIBE DRAM _____

FRUGAL BEET _____

OVERUSE FOLLY _____

BEE TILT _____

HIKE TAMP PANE _____

INK BED _____

FUSIBLE LIEU FIAT _____

THRONG INTEGER _____

LOUSY FOE RUDE _____

ARGUE YOU HONE _____

SAUCY YE ON _____

OVEN WON ERR _____

GUYS HI TOOT _____

BEHAVES DINGO POP _____

JEJUNE HONEY TROY _____

ROB TIN GIN _____

HELIX HA AN LEE _____

ANAGRAMS
Simply unscramble the words.

Happy Travels

GUT GALE GAG _____

SOAKING WELSH _____

REROUTING OPAL _____

BARGAINS PODS _____

PROPHETS DORSAL _____

EERILY TUNICA _____

TURBINE SLAM _____

CHIRP ISSUE _____

NIX SOURCE _____

MAGPIE GIRL _____

CABAL BAITS _____

STREWN DUAL _____

GOLD GIN _____

OVARIES RENT _____

ANTACID COO MOMS _____

NOVA BOGEY _____

FAWN RETORT _____

AGE PRAY _____

TRINKET CUTER _____

MOMS OWING LIP _____

BE **YOURSELF**

I am someone who:

Loves _____

Hates _____

Dreams of _____

Is determined to _____

Is scared of _____

Is inspired by _____

Is grateful for _____

Has a habit of _____

Is happiest when _____

Is angry when _____

Is sad when _____

Is nervous when _____

Is hopeful for _____

Laughs when _____

Cries when _____

Freaks out when _____

Believes in _____

In the future will _____

BE **YOURSELF**

Write 10 interesting and/or unusual things about yourself.

1. _____

2. _____

3. _____

4. _____

5. _____

6. _____

7. _____

8. _____

9. _____

10. _____

What is your favorite word and why?

_____

_____

_____

_____

_____

_____

BE **YOURSELF**

Write your life story in 25 sentences or less.

_____

_____

_____

_____

_____

_____

_____

_____

_____

_____

_____

_____

_____

_____

_____

"Don't listen
to what they say. **Go see**."
- Unknown

BE **YOURSELF**

Top five pet peeves.

1. _____

2. _____

3. _____

4. _____

5. _____

10 things that make you smile.

1. _____

2. _____

3. _____

4. _____

5. _____

6. _____

7. _____

8. _____

9. _____

10. _____

BE **YOURSELF**

30 places you REALLY want to visit.

1. _____ 16. _____

2. _____ 17. _____

3. _____ 18. _____

4. _____ 19. _____

5. _____ 20. _____

6. _____ 21. _____

7. _____ 22. _____

8. _____ 23. _____

9. _____ 24. _____

10. _____ 25. _____

11. _____ 26. _____

12. _____ 27. _____

13. _____ 28. _____

14. _____ 29. _____

15. _____ 30. _____

100 Things I REALLY Love

For this one you're going to make a "list of lists" that will all add up to 100 things that you absolutely LOVE. Make sure to give a brief explanation for each of the items on your list. For example, don't just list your favorite city; write about what you love so much about it such as the late night eats, the cobble stone streets, the live music scene, etc.

10 Activities

1. _____

2. _____

3. _____

4. _____

5. _____

6. _____

7. _____

8. _____

9. _____

10. _____

"Patience
is the companion of wisdom."
St. Augustine

100 Things I REALLY Love

10 Restaurants

1. _____
2. _____
3. _____
4. _____
5. _____
6. _____
7. _____
8. _____
9. _____
10. _____

10 People

1. _____ 6. _____
2. _____ 7. _____
3. _____ 8. _____
4. _____ 9. _____
5. _____ 10. _____

100 Things I REALLY Love

10 Foods

1. _____
2. _____
3. _____
4. _____
5. _____

6. _____
7. _____
8. _____
9. _____
10. _____

5 Drinks

1. _____
2. _____
3. _____
4. _____
5. _____

5 Desserts

6. _____
7. _____
8. _____
9. _____
10. _____

10 Cities

1. _____
2. _____
3. _____
4. _____
5. _____

6. _____
7. _____
8. _____
9. _____
10. _____

100 Things I REALLY Love

10 Historical Sites/Landmarks/Parks

1. _____
2. _____
3. _____
4. _____
5. _____
6. _____
7. _____
8. _____
9. _____
10. _____

5 Websites

1. _____
2. _____
3. _____
4. _____
5. _____

"**Once a year**,
go someplace
you've never been before."
- Dalai Lama

100 Things I REALLY Love

5 Podcasts or Apps

1. _____
2. _____
3. _____
4. _____
5. _____

5 Books

1. _____
2. _____
3. _____
4. _____
5. _____

5 Writers

1. _____
2. _____
3. _____
4. _____
5. _____

100 Things I REALLY Love

5 Movies

1. _____
2. _____
3. _____
4. _____
5. _____

5 Songs

1. _____
2. _____
3. _____
4. _____
5. _____

Simply fill in the blanks...

I am a _____ person with an awesome

_____. My best _____ is my

_____. I make people _____ with

my _____. I work hard to be the _____

in the world. My favorite _____ is _____.

But, I really don't like _____ or _____.

Someday I'll make it to _____ to see _____.

If I could _____ only one thing, it would be

_____. I _____ more than

_____. _____ is something I would

never _____. I can _____ the most

amazing _____. The _____ place I have

been to is _____. My _____ would describe

me as _____. I first _____ when I was

_____. My last _____ was

_____.

Favorite Things from *A to Z*

A _____   N _____

B _____   O _____

C _____   P _____

D _____   Q _____

E _____   R _____

F _____   S _____

G _____   T _____

H _____   U _____

I _____   V _____

J _____   W _____

K _____   X _____

L _____   Y _____

M _____   Z _____

BE **CALM**

MANTRA

A mantra is a word or a sound meant to be chanted aloud or repeated silently in order to enhance concentration. It can be broken down into two parts: "man" which means mind, and "tra" which means transport or vehicle. *(So in short, a mantra is an instrument of the mind – a powerful sound or vibration - that you can use to enter a deep state of meditation).*

How many times should you repeat a mantra? Well, that depends on the length of the mantra. Shorter mantras should be chanted 108 times (it's considered a sacred number in Hinduism and Buddhism). But, if you're in a hurry, you can chant it either 11 or 21 times. Longer ones can be repeated up to three times. *Tip: Mala beads can help you with your counting.*

BE **CALM**

OM

Chances are you've probably heard this mantra, especially if you've ever been to a yoga class.

Om – or AUM, pronounced "Aaaa—Uooo—Mmm," is an ancient mantra that is commonly used in Hinduism and Buddhism, but is easily accessible to anyone, regardless of faith or religion. It is considered to have a very high spiritual and creative power and is believed to be the first sound that emerged from the vibrations of the cosmic energy that created the universe.

Recent scientific studies have shown that chanting Om can calm both your body and your mind, helping to bring you into the present moment and become more mindful. Namaste.

BE CALM

── Om Mani Padme Hum ──

Om Mani Padme Hum is one of the most popular mantras in the world. It's used by Tibetan Buddhists to invoke Chenrezig, the Bodhisattva embodiment of compassion and mercy. Literally, this chant translates to "Hail the jewel in the lotus."

However, the exact meaning of the mantra cannot be so easily conveyed in just a few sentences, as the mantra is the essence of the entire teachings of Buddha. But here's a rough guide to breaking it down:

Om – Purifies ego.

Ma – Purifies jealousy.

Ni – Purifies passion.

Pad – Purifies ignorance.

Me – Purifies greed.

Hum – Purifies hatred.

BE **CALM**

Ham-Sa

Ham and Sa in Sanskrit translates to "I am he/that". This **mantra reaffirms that we can (and should) be fully present in** each moment, knowing that it is only temporary and also that we are not alone.

Whatever our current circumstance – stuck in a long line at **airport security, fighting with a loved one, feeling lonely or** homesick, etc. - things will change again in the next instant and we will be there as well, coping as best that we can. And so will every other person on this earth.

Just simply inhale on the "Hahhhhhm" and exhale on the "Sahhhhh." Ahhh, don't you feel better already?

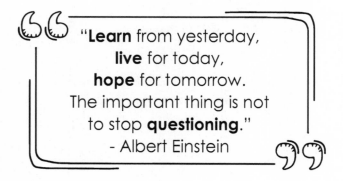

"**Learn** from yesterday,
live for today,
hope for tomorrow.
The important thing is not
to stop **questioning**."
- Albert Einstein

BE **PRESENT**
and
BREATHE

Breathing. It seems so simple and mundane, but most of us are actually doing it wrong. The good news is that once you learn how to do it correctly (think deeper, longer breaths), there's almost nothing that it can't help.

Good, deep breathing increases energy, improves the respiratory system, calms the nervous system, strengthens the lymphatic system, releases muscle tension, improves the cardiovascular system, elevates the digestive system, and relax the mind and boost our ability to learn, focus and concentrate.

Here are a few breathing exercises to help you chill out and become more centered.

"Equal Breathing" or Sama Vritti

Sit in a comfortable, cross-legged position. If this isn't an option, simply lie on your back or sit in a chair. Whatever feels best.

Close your eyes and breathe in slowly for a count of four; pause; then breathe out for a count of four (all through the nose). Repeat this several times. If it feels comfortable after a few cycles, you can try expanding to a count of five, six or even eight counts per breath.

Benefit: calms the nervous system, increases focus and helps reduce stress. Great to do before bedtime.

"Alternate Nostril Breathing"
or
Nadi Shodhana

Start in a comfortable seated position, spine straight.
Rest your left palm gently on your left knee, bringing your
right hand towards your nose.

Using your right thumb, softly close off your right nostril and
inhale deeply through your left nostril. At the peak of
**inhalation, pause, then softly close off your left nostril with
your ring finger (or pinky finger if that's easier) and exhale**
slowly through your right nostril.

Inhale slowly through your right nostril, pause, then close it
with the thumb. Exhale through your left nostril. Once your
exhalation is complete, inhale slowly through the left. Pause
before moving to your right nostril. Repeat this pattern five
to ten times. Then release your right hand to your right knee
and begin to ease back into normal breathing.

Benefit: restores balance in the left and right hemispheres of
the brain and helps rejuvenate the nervous system. Great
when you're stressed out and/or anxious.

4-7-8 Breathing Technique

Sit with your back straight, either on the floor or in a chair. Place the tip of your tongue behind your upper front teeth, and keep it there throughout the entire exercise. You will be exhaling through your mouth, around your tongue. You can try pursing your lips slightly if this feels awkward.

To begin, exhale completely through your mouth, making a whoosh sound. Then close your mouth and inhale quietly through your nose to a count of four. Hold your breath for a count of seven. Then exhale completely through your mouth, making a whoosh sound to a count of eight. This is one breath. Now inhale again and repeat the cycle three more times for a total of four breaths.

Benefit: according to integrative medicine expert Dr. Andrew Weil, this breathing exercise is "a natural tranquilizer for the nervous system" and eases the body into a state of calmness and relaxation. Great for any time of day.

"Lion's Breath"
or
Simhasana Pranayama

This one can be done in almost any pose, including in a cross-legged position or lying down. Yogi's choice.

Begin by inhaling slowly through your nose. Then exhale strongly through the mouth, making a "ha" sound. As you exhale, open your mouth wide (really wide!) and stick your tongue out as far as possible. Try bringing your focus towards your third eye (center of your forehead) or the tip of your nose as you exhale. Repeat four to six times.

Benefit: increased energy and it also helps relieve tension and stress by stretching your entire face, including your jaw and tongue. Great addition to your morning routine.

BE **GRATEFUL**

How Was Your Day?

Greatest accomplishment _____

Tastiest bite or beverage _____

Loveliest sight _____

Coolest conversation _____

Major highlight _____

One wish _____

Most grateful for _____

BE **GRATEFUL**

How Was Your Day?

Greatest accomplishment _____

Tastiest bite or beverage _____

Loveliest sight _____

Coolest conversation _____

Major highlight _____

One wish _____

Most grateful for _____

BE **GRATEFUL**

How Was Your Day?

Greatest accomplishment _____

Tastiest bite or beverage _____

Loveliest sight _____

Coolest conversation _____

Major highlight _____

One wish _____

Most grateful for _____

BE **GRATEFUL**

How Was Your Day?

Greatest accomplishment _____

Tastiest bite or beverage _____

Loveliest sight _____

Coolest conversation _____

Major highlight _____

One wish _____

Most grateful for _____

"If **dream** it,
you can **do** it."

BE **GRATEFUL**

How Was Your Day?

Greatest accomplishment _____

Tastiest bite or beverage _____

Loveliest sight _____

Coolest conversation _____

Major highlight _____

One wish _____

Most grateful for _____

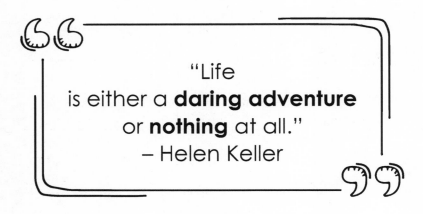

"Life
is either a **daring adventure**
or **nothing** at all."
– Helen Keller

BE **GRATEFUL**

How Was Your Day?

Greatest accomplishment _____

Tastiest bite or beverage _____

Loveliest sight _____

Coolest conversation _____

Major highlight _____

One wish _____

Most grateful for _____

BE **GRATEFUL**

How Was Your Day?

Greatest accomplishment _____

Tastiest bite or beverage _____

Loveliest sight _____

Coolest conversation _____

Major highlight _____

One wish _____

Most grateful for _____

BE **GRATEFUL**

How Was Your Day?

Greatest accomplishment _____

Tastiest bite or beverage _____

Loveliest sight _____

Coolest conversation _____

Major highlight _____

One wish _____

Most grateful for _____

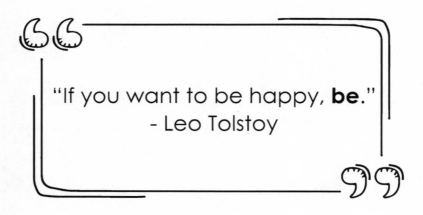

"If you want to be happy, **be**."
- Leo Tolstoy

BE **GRATEFUL**

How Was Your Day?

Greatest accomplishment _____

Tastiest bite or beverage _____

Loveliest sight _____

Coolest conversation _____

Major highlight _____

One wish _____

Most grateful for _____

BE **GRATEFUL**

How Was Your Day?

Greatest accomplishment _____

Tastiest bite or beverage _____

Loveliest sight _____

Coolest conversation _____

Major highlight _____

One wish _____

Most grateful for _____

BE **GRATEFUL**

How Was Your Day?

Greatest accomplishment _____

Tastiest bite or beverage _____

Loveliest sight _____

Coolest conversation _____

Major highlight _____

One wish _____

Most grateful for _____

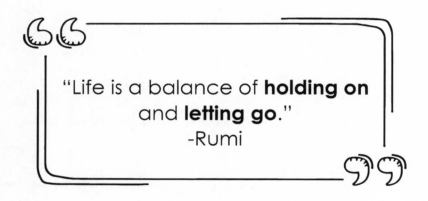

"Life is a balance of **holding on** and **letting go**."
-Rumi

BE **GRATEFUL**

How Was Your Day?

Greatest accomplishment _____

Tastiest bite or beverage _____

Loveliest sight _____

Coolest conversation _____

Major highlight _____

One wish _____

Most grateful for _____

BE **GRATEFUL**

How Was Your Day?

Greatest accomplishment _____

Tastiest bite or beverage _____

Loveliest sight _____

Coolest conversation _____

Major highlight _____

One wish _____

Most grateful for _____

BE **GRATEFUL**

How Was Your Day?

Greatest accomplishment _____

Tastiest bite or beverage _____

Loveliest sight _____

Coolest conversation _____

Major highlight _____

One wish _____

Most grateful for _____

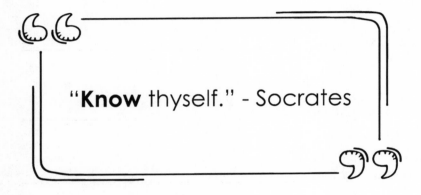

"**Know** thyself." - Socrates

BE **GRATEFUL**

How Was Your Day?

Greatest accomplishment _____

Tastiest bite or beverage _____

Loveliest sight _____

Coolest conversation _____

Major highlight _____

One wish _____

Most grateful for _____

BE **GRATEFUL**

How Was Your Day?

Greatest accomplishment _____

Tastiest bite or beverage _____

Loveliest sight _____

Coolest conversation _____

Major highlight _____

One wish _____

Most grateful for _____

BE **GRATEFUL**

How Was Your Day?

Greatest accomplishment _____

Tastiest bite or beverage _____

Loveliest sight _____

Coolest conversation _____

Major highlight _____

One wish _____

Most grateful for _____

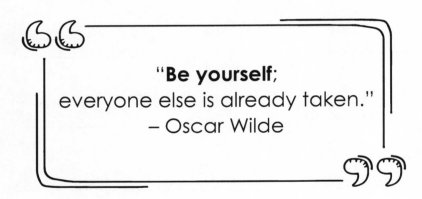

"**Be yourself**;
everyone else is already taken."
– Oscar Wilde

BE **GRATEFUL**

How Was Your Day?

Greatest accomplishment _____

Tastiest bite or beverage _____

Loveliest sight _____

Coolest conversation _____

Major highlight _____

One wish _____

Most grateful for _____

BE **GRATEFUL**

How Was Your Day?

Greatest accomplishment _____

Tastiest bite or beverage _____

Loveliest sight _____

Coolest conversation _____

Major highlight _____

One wish _____

Most grateful for _____

BE **GRATEFUL**

How Was Your Day?

Greatest accomplishment _____

Tastiest bite or beverage _____

Loveliest sight _____

Coolest conversation _____

Major highlight _____

One wish _____

Most grateful for _____

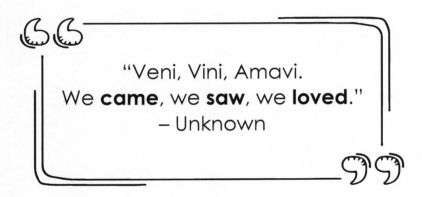

"Veni, Vini, Amavi.
We **came**, we **saw**, we **loved**."
– Unknown

BE **GRATEFUL**

How Was Your Day?

Greatest accomplishment _____

Tastiest bite or beverage _____

Loveliest sight _____

Coolest conversation _____

Major highlight _____

One wish _____

Most grateful for _____

BE **GRATEFUL**

How Was Your Day?

Greatest accomplishment _____

Tastiest bite or beverage _____

Loveliest sight _____

Coolest conversation _____

Major highlight _____

One wish _____

Most grateful for _____

BE **GRATEFUL**

How Was Your Day?

Greatest accomplishment _____

Tastiest bite or beverage _____

Loveliest sight _____

Coolest conversation _____

Major highlight _____

One wish _____

Most grateful for _____

Do not dwell in the past,
do not **dream** of the future,
concentrate the mind on
the present moment."
– Buddha

BE **GRATEFUL**

How Was Your Day?

Greatest accomplishment _____

Tastiest bite or beverage _____

Loveliest sight _____

Coolest conversation _____

Major highlight _____

One wish _____

Most grateful for _____

BE **GRATEFUL**

How Was Your Day?

Greatest accomplishment _____

Tastiest bite or beverage _____

Loveliest sight _____

Coolest conversation _____

Major highlight _____

One wish _____

Most grateful for _____

BE **GRATEFUL**

How Was Your Day?

Greatest accomplishment _____

Tastiest bite or beverage _____

Loveliest sight _____

Coolest conversation _____

Major highlight _____

One wish _____

Most grateful for _____

BE **GRATEFUL**

How Was Your Day?

Greatest accomplishment _____

Tastiest bite or beverage _____

Loveliest sight _____

Coolest conversation _____

Major highlight _____

One wish _____

Most grateful for _____

BE **GRATEFUL**

How Was Your Day?

Greatest accomplishment _____

Tastiest bite or beverage _____

Loveliest sight _____

Coolest conversation _____

Major highlight _____

One wish _____

Most grateful for _____

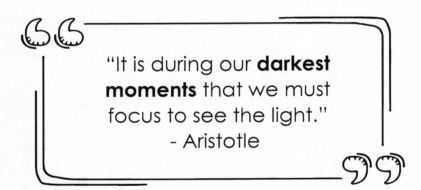

"It is during our **darkest moments** that we must focus to see the light."
- Aristotle

BE A **VISIONARY**

Health/Welness

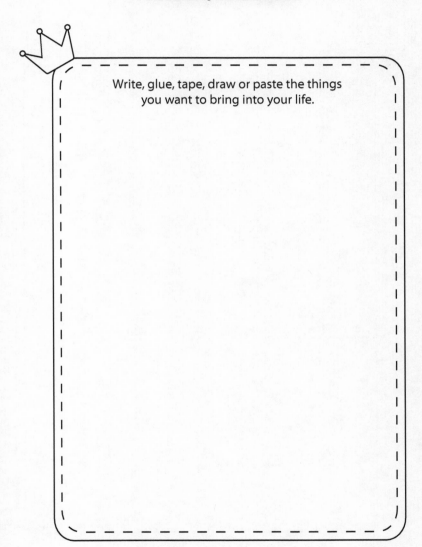

Write, glue, tape, draw or paste the things
you want to bring into your life.

BE A **VISIONARY**

Family

Write, glue, tape, draw or paste the things
you want to bring into your life.

BE A **VISIONARY**

Money

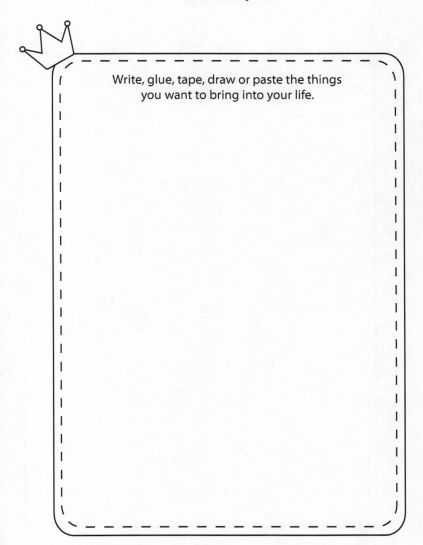

Write, glue, tape, draw or paste the things
you want to bring into your life.

BE A **VISIONARY**

Work

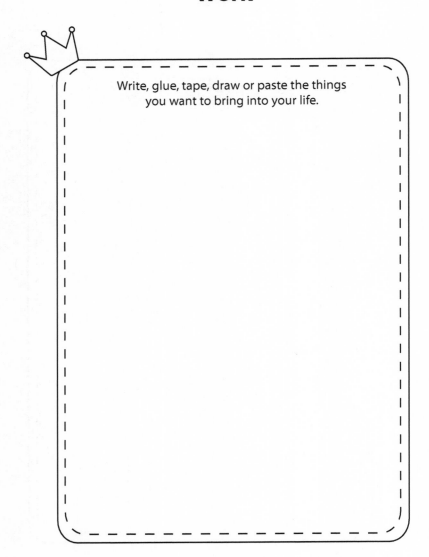

Write, glue, tape, draw or paste the things
you want to bring into your life.

BE A **VISIONARY**

Relationships

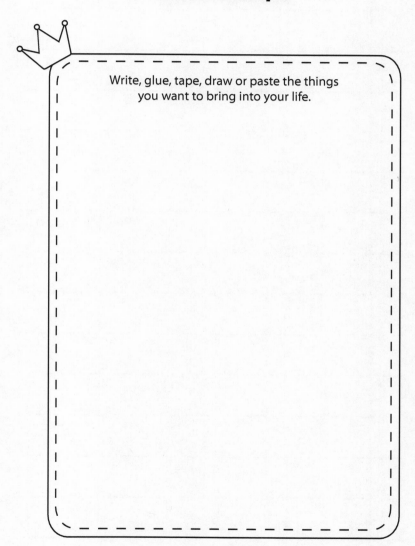

Write, glue, tape, draw or paste the things
you want to bring into your life.

NOTES

NOTES

NOTES

NOTES

NOTES

NOTES

NOTES

NOTES

NOTES

NOTES

_____

_____

_____

_____

_____

_____

_____

_____

_____

_____

_____

_____

NOTES

NOTES

NOTES

NOTES

NOTES

NOTES

TO DO

_____

_____

_____

_____

_____

_____

_____

_____

_____

_____

_____

_____

TO DO

TO DO

TO DO

TO DO

_____

_____

_____

_____

_____

_____

_____

_____

_____

_____

_____

_____

_____

TO DO

TO DO

TO DO

TO DO

TO DO

_____

_____

_____

_____

_____

_____

_____

_____

_____

_____

_____

_____

TO DO

_____

_____

_____

_____

_____

_____

_____

_____

_____

_____

_____

_____

_____

TO DO

TO DO

TO DO

TO DO

SOLUTIONS

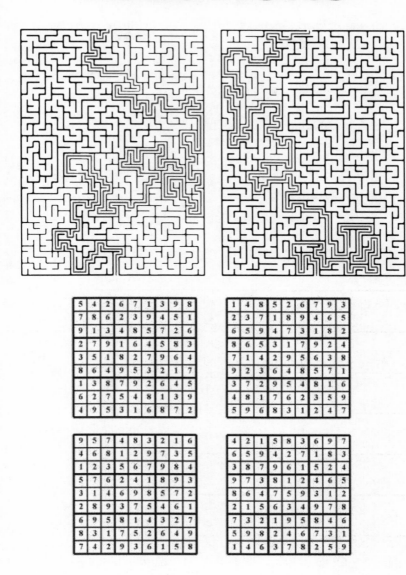

5	4	2	6	7	1	3	9	8
7	8	6	2	3	9	4	5	1
9	1	3	4	8	5	7	2	6
2	7	9	1	6	4	5	8	3
3	5	1	8	2	7	9	6	4
8	6	4	9	5	3	2	1	7
1	3	8	7	9	2	6	4	5
6	2	7	5	4	8	1	3	9
4	9	5	3	1	6	8	7	2

1	4	8	5	2	6	7	9	3
2	3	7	1	8	9	4	6	5
6	5	9	4	7	3	1	8	2
8	6	5	3	1	7	9	2	4
7	1	4	2	9	5	6	3	8
9	2	3	6	4	8	5	7	1
3	7	2	9	5	4	8	1	6
4	8	1	7	6	2	3	5	9
5	9	6	8	3	1	2	4	7

9	5	7	4	8	3	2	1	6
4	6	8	1	2	9	7	3	5
1	2	3	5	6	7	9	8	4
5	7	6	2	4	1	8	9	3
3	1	4	6	9	8	5	7	2
2	8	9	3	7	5	4	6	1
6	9	5	8	1	4	3	2	7
8	3	1	7	5	2	6	4	9
7	4	2	9	3	6	1	5	8

4	2	1	5	8	3	6	9	7
6	5	9	4	2	7	1	8	3
3	8	7	9	6	1	5	2	4
9	7	3	8	1	2	4	6	5
8	6	4	7	5	9	3	1	2
2	1	5	6	3	4	9	7	8
7	3	2	1	9	5	8	4	6
5	9	8	2	4	6	7	3	1
1	4	6	3	7	8	2	5	9

ANAGRAM ANSWER KEY

Inspirational Phrases

CHOOSE JOY

BE BRAVE

YOU ARE LOVELY

DREAM BIG

BE GRATEFUL

LOVE YOURSELF

LET IT BE

MAKE IT HAPPEN

BE KIND

LIFE IS BEAUTIFUL

REGRET NOTHING

FEED YOUR SOUL

YOU ARE ENOUGH

YES YOU CAN

NOW OR NEVER

YOU GOT THIS

GOOD VIBES HAPPEN

ENJOY THE JOURNEY

BRING IT ON

INHALE EXHALE

Happy Travels

LUGGAGE TAG

WALKING SHOES

AIRPORT LOUNGE

BOARDING PASS

PASSPORT HOLDER

SECURITY LINE

BUS TERMINAL

CRUISE SHIP

EXCURSION

PILGRIMAGE

SABBATICAL

WANDERLUST

LODGING

RESERVATION

ACCOMMODATIONS

BON VOYAGE

WATERFRONT

GAP YEAR

RETURN TICKET

SWIMMING POOL

ACKNOWLEDGMENTS

My warmest thanks go out to all the people who helped me design, proofread and edit this book. You know who you are. And I am forever grateful.

ABOUT THE AUTHOR

Susan Wildes is a **writer** and **travel junkie**.
She currently lives in Mexico.

Made in the USA
Middletown, DE
20 December 2019